D1100635

Motivation in the Workplace:
Inspiring Your Employees

Lydia Banks

American Media Publishing
4900 University Avenue
West Des Moines, Iowa 50266-6769
800-262-2557

000139687

Motivation in the Workplace:
Inspiring Your Employees

Lydia Banks
Copyright 1997 by American Media Incorporated

Credits:

American Media Publishing:	Arthur Bauer
	Todd McDonald
Managing Editor:	Karen Massetti Miller
Designer:	Gayle O'Brien

Published by American Media Inc., 4900 University Avenue
West Des Moines, IA 50266-6769

Library of Congress Card Number 97-070993
Banks, Lydia
Motivation in the Workplace: Inspiring Your Employees

Printed in the United States of America
ISBN 1-884926-46-0

Introduction

Inspiring employee motivation requires much more than the old-fashioned carrot-and-stick approach. Today's manager needs to understand the reasons why employees work and offer the rewards they hope to receive.

This book will introduce you to the many factors that affect employee motivation. As you read, you'll discover:

◆ What employees expect from work (it's more than just money)

◆ How a manager's vision and values inspire employees

◆ Effective ways to reward your employees

◆ The importance of creating a supportive workplace

◆ The role open communication plays in maintaining motivation

◆ How to deal with unmotivated employees

By the time you're done, you'll be ready to inspire your employees in dozens of ways and create a work environment that will support their desire to achieve.

● Table of Contents

Chapter *One*

What Is Motivation?

Chapter Objectives

▶ Understand the nature of employee motivation.

▶ Recognize the importance of creating a workplace that inspires and supports employee motivation.

▶ Identify aspects of today's workplace that can affect employee motivation.

Managers can create an environment that inspires and supports employee motivation.

M ost of us have seen people who perform their jobs by doing as little as possible. They come to work late and leave early. They miss deadlines, and when they complete a task, they do only the minimum required. They can often be found spending some extra time in the break room complaining about their jobs.

We also know people who give 110 percent to any project. They're punctual and hardworking, and they approach new projects with a smile instead of a complaint. What makes these two types of workers so different? The answer is *motivation*.

Motivated employees have a will to succeed, a drive to do their best no matter what the project. Unmotivated employees are less concerned about their performance and willing to get by with a minimum amount of effort.

As a manager, you want to develop and encourage good employee performance, and good performance comes from strong employee motivation. But managers can't *motivate* employees. Motivation is an internal state, like emotions and attitudes, that only the individual can control. Managers can, however, create a workplace environment that will inspire and support strong motivation on the part of employees. That is what we will explore in this book. Specifically, we will consider how managers can:

◆ Create a workplace that helps employees satisfy psychological needs as well as the need for income.

◆ Set clear goals for employee performance.

◆ Encourage good performance through rewards and reinforcement.

◆ Maintain open communication with all employees.

We will explore these techniques in the following chapters. But before we begin, let's take a look at some of the unique features of today's workplace and how those features affect motivation.

Take a Moment

Think of a situation in which you felt motivated to do your very best. Can you identify any aspect of that situation that inspired and supported your motivation? Describe it below:

_____

_____

_____

_____

_____

Motivation in Today's Workplace

Motivation in today's workplace is affected by a number of factors, including:

◆ A decreasing emphasis on money.

◆ An increasing amount of work.

◆ An increasing need to work together in teams.

Placing Less Emphasis on Money

For many years, conventional wisdom held that employees worked primarily for money and could be "motivated" through a combination of financial reward and fear. Within this perspective, employers might offer a financial reward as their only performance incentive, or they might try to generate fear by threatening to fire or demote employees if they did not perform at a certain level.

Today, we realize that our reasons for performing well on the job are far more complex. Though we often define a good job as a good-paying job, many of us would also consider other issues, such as job satisfaction and time for a family life.

Patrick is a case in point. When he began his job as a pharmaceutical sales representative, he was excited about the job's high salary. He pounded the pavement every day and spent much of his free time thinking of new ways to generate new sales. The hard work paid off, and Patrick rose through the ranks, getting more pay, more commissions, and many bonuses.

As Patrick's income grew, so did his family's possessions. First, they bought a new car, then a new house, then new furniture for every room. Patrick worked, worked, worked, and he bought more, more, more.

But after a few years, Patrick began to be dissatisfied. He had everything that money could buy, but he barely saw his family all week, and he was getting tired of sales. He longed for new challenges and time to spend with his children before they grew up and left home.

> **Though we often define a good job as a good-paying job, many of us would also consider other issues, such as job satisfaction and time for a family life.**

Situations like Patrick's are more common than you might think. Many of today's workers are not primarily motivated by a desire for money. They crave a deeper satisfaction from their jobs and won't respond to old-style management techniques.

Take a Moment

Why do you work? Does the thought of more money inspire you to do your best, or do other rewards inspire you more? List some of the factors that help you increase your motivation.

_____

_____

_____

_____

_____

Dealing with Greater Amounts of Work

One of the primary challenges facing today's worker is an increased workload. Workforces have been downsized. Technology has pushed us to a faster pace. The result is that employees must learn a variety of new tasks and use their minds and bodies at a faster rate than ever before. Though these changes may bring many benefits, the stress involved in any change can affect employee motivation.

One of the primary challenges facing today's worker is an increased workload.

Take a Moment

Have increased workloads or changes in tasks affected your staff in the past year or two? List some of the effects you've noticed below:

_____

_____

_____

_____

_____

For many workers, home life can be just as busy as the workplace.

For many workers, home life can be just as busy as the workplace. Completing housework and laundry, juggling day care, preparing meals, and supervising homework can create what amounts to a second workday at home. Because many baby boomers married and started families late in life, they may be faced with the added challenge of raising small children at the same time that they are given increased managerial responsibilities.

Here is a log of a typical evening compiled by a married employee with young children. It was created to illustrate how much activity a parent can encounter after a long day at work.

5:25 p.m.	Pick up Annie at day care.
5:45	Pick up Jonathan at after-school care.
6:00	Arrive home. Set table as children wash hands.
6:12	Answer phone; salesperson calling.
6:13	Help Annie, who has slipped on bathroom floor.
6:14	Look at Jonathan's schoolwork while getting out food and pouring drinks.
6:18	Greet spouse, who complains about fast-food dinner.
6:20	Settle fight after Annie throws french fries at Jonathan.
6:25	Answer phone. Mother asks when family is coming to visit.

To continue would take up several pages of this book! It's easy to see how an employee so busy at home could feel tired and unmotivated at work.

1

Take a Moment

Is your home life as busy as the example above? Keep a log of a typical evening; then log a typical morning. How does your home life affect your work life? Do you think other employees in your department have similar concerns?

_____

_____

_____

_____

_____

Working in Teams

The amount of work isn't the only aspect of the workplace that has recently changed—the way people work together has changed as well. Today's workers are increasingly asked to work in teams, and this can have both positive and negative effects on motivation. If employees are able to build a strong team relationship, their shared sense of commitment can inspire motivation on the part of individual members. But if the team experiences a number of conflicts, or if individual members believe their efforts are ignored or undervalued, these poor dynamics could discourage motivation.

Working in teams can have both positive and negative effects on motivation.

Take a Moment

Does your organization or department have a number of work teams? If so, how do you think team dynamics are affecting the motivation of individual team members?

_____

_____

_____

_____

Encouraging the Desire to Succeed

This book takes the perspective that people are inherently well-meaning and *want* to do a good job. Even those people who currently perform their duties in a lackluster manner have some desire for success; it simply isn't manifesting itself in their job situation.

By providing the right kind of support, managers can develop and encourage employees' will to succeed. But employees must bring something to the equation as well: open minds and the willingness to work with management to make changes that will improve the workplace and their own performance. Working together, management and employees can create an environment in which everyone feels motivated to give every challenge her or his best effort.

> By providing the right kind of support, managers can develop and encourage employees' will to succeed.

1

Summary

Motivated employees have a drive to succeed no matter what the project. Managers cannot "motivate" employees, but they can create an environment that inspires and supports strong employee motivation.

As managers strive to create a good work environment, they should be aware of several features of today's workplace that can affect employee motivation:

◆ A decreasing emphasis on money

◆ An increasing amount of work

◆ An increasing need to work together in teams

By taking these and other factors into account, managers can create an environment that encourages employees' desire to succeed. Employees must also contribute to this effort by keeping an open mind and working with management to improve the work environment and their own performance.

Motivated employees have a drive to succeed no matter what the project.

Self-Check: Chapter 1 Review

Answers to these questions appear on page 108.

1. True or False?
   Managers can motivate employees.

2. Today's workers place a decreasing emphasis on

   _____.

3. True or false?
   Fear is an effective way to encourage motivation.

4. For many workers, home life and the workplace are

   equally _____.

5. Team situations can inspire employee motivation when

   _____.

   They can discourage employee motivation when

   _____.

Chapter *Two*

Why Do We Work?

Chapter Objectives

▶ Understand the nature of employee motivation.

▶ Recognize the importance of creating a workplace that inspires and supports employee motivation.

▶ Identify aspects of today's workplace that can affect employee motivation.

Why do we work? What makes us struggle out of bed every morning, stumble through breakfast, and fight rush hour traffic, when it would be so much easier to spend the day in front of the TV with a bowl of popcorn?

The more needs our jobs can help us meet, the more our motivation to perform well is encouraged.

Survival is part of the answer. We work to eat, buy clothes, pay our rent or mortgage. But survival is only one of the reasons we work. We work in order to meet many different needs, and the more needs our jobs can help us meet, the more our motivation to perform well is encouraged. Understanding why people work and what needs they hope to fill can help managers determine what they can do to appeal to those needs and inspire employee motivation.

Take a Moment

Why do you think you work? Is survival the only reason, or do you work for something more? List some of the reasons you work below:

_____

_____

_____

_____

2

What Are Our Needs?

Humans are complex creatures with a variety of needs. Some of our needs, like the need for air, water, food, and shelter, are basic and necessary for physical survival. Others, like the need for love and companionship, are psychological and emotional. One useful model for categorizing human needs was developed by Abraham Maslow. As you can see in the figure below, Maslow organized human needs into a hierarchy with the needs most basic to survival on the bottom. Maslow suggested that once those basic needs are filled, people can progress up the hierarchy to focus on emotional satisfaction and self-fulfillment.

Some of our needs are basic and necessary for physical survival; others are psychological and emotional.

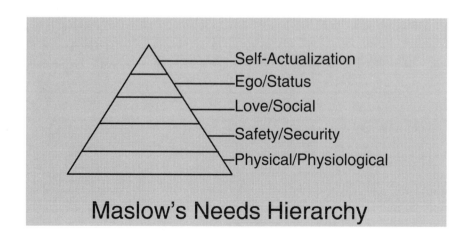

Maslow's Needs Hierarchy

- Self-Actualization
- Ego/Status
- Love/Social
- Safety/Security
- Physical/Physiological

We have many different ways of filling the categories of needs described by Maslow. Here are some ways they are met in modern society.

Need	Description	How Need Is Met in Modern Society
Physical/Physiological	Elements needed for physical survival	Clean air and water, sleep, sex
Safety/Security	Protection from harm	Shelter, warning systems, security systems, laws, and law enforcement
Love/Social	Companionship and affection	Social groups, social events, shared tasks, mating, family
Ego/Status	Position in social group	Position in family, community, or work; feeling of self-worth
Self-Actualization	Feeling of achieving one's best	Education, therapy, meditation, decision-making power, control over one's life, ability to produce desired outcomes

Take a Moment

Go over the categories of human needs and how they can be filled. Can you think of ways in which the workplace can help people meet these needs? List them below:

Physical/Physiological _____

Safety/Security _____

Love/Social_____

Ego/Status _____

Self-Actualization _____

Though this list of the ways our needs can be met is by no means exhaustive, you may have already begun to see its relationship to the workplace. When employees' needs for food, shelter, security, and status are met, they will feel more motivated than when those needs are not met. Employers can meet employee needs in a number of ways, through income and the work environment itself.

Meeting Needs Through Income

Employees with steady incomes can meet physical needs for food and shelter and security needs for clean, safe neighborhoods. A good-sized income can help employees acquire items that help them meet status needs, such as a new car or a bigger house, and give employees the leisure time to pursue self-actualization through hobbies or other forms of self-expression.

As we will discuss later in this chapter, employers can use income in many ways to inspire motivation. But income isn't the only way the workplace can fill employee needs. The work environment itself can satisfy many employee needs.

Meeting Needs Through Work Environment

The following list includes just a few ways in which employee needs may be satisfied at work:

◆ **Physical needs**—A workplace meets employees' physical needs by providing comfortable work spaces with clean air and good lighting. Even the most positive attitude can be damaged by a dark, uncomfortable work environment.

◆ **Security needs**—Employees who are worried about their physical safety can't concentrate on work. Employers can meet employee security needs by taking precautions against violence, harassment, and physical danger. Employers can also meet employee security needs by protecting jobs through fair personnel and salary decisions and by providing extra incentives, such as on-site day care for employees' children or lists of certified child-care providers.

When employees' needs for food, shelter, security, and status are met, they will feel more motivated than when those needs are not met.

19

◆ **Social needs**—Though employers don't pay workers to socialize, many social needs can be met at work through the opportunity to work on teams and participate in group activities. Strong team relationships encourage strong employee motivation.

◆ **Ego/Status**—Work offers the possibility of promotion and the opportunity to progress through various ranks and salary levels. Employees are much more motivated to work when they don't perceive themselves as holding "dead end" jobs.

At its best, work provides employees with interesting assignments that allow them to grow professionally and personally.

◆ **Self-Actualization**—At its best, work provides employees with interesting assignments that allow them to grow professionally and personally. As employees become self-actualized, they accept more responsibility for their performance and receive more control over their activities.

One final way that the workplace can help employees meet their needs is by providing them the flexibility to take care of issues in other areas of their lives. As Maslow's list of needs suggests, our work and personal lives are not as neatly separated as we might like.

An employee whose security needs are threatened by a lack of good day care at home will not be as motivated as an employee whose day care needs are met. Flexible scheduling can inspire employee motivation by giving employees the freedom to resolve personal problems before coming to work.

Take a Moment

Can you think of some ways in which your organization currently fills employee needs? List them below. Can you think of any additional ways it might fill employee needs in the future? List those too.

Needs

How my organization helps/could help fill those needs

Physical/
Physiological

_____

_____

Safety/Security

_____

_____

Love/Social

_____

_____

Ego/Status

_____

_____

Self-Actualization

_____

_____

Other Work-Based Needs

Psychologist David McClelland provides another way of categorizing the needs people hope to satisfy through their work. He identified three types of work-based needs:

1. The need for affiliation

2. The need for achievement

3. The need for power

According to McClelland, not everyone has the same level of need for each particular area. A dominant type of person might have a strong need for power, a secondary need for achievement, but little need for affiliation. The sociable worker's greatest need be for affiliation rather than power. A worker with low self-esteem might focus on achievement but be too shy to seek power or affiliation.

Once again, there are numerous ways in which employers might help employees meet these needs, including:

◆ Creating work teams to increase the opportunity for affiliation.

◆ Developing challenging work assignments that will increase the opportunity for achievement.

◆ Giving employees more control over their own work situations as a means of empowerment.

Take a Moment

How would you rank your work-based needs? Use a scale of 1, 2, and 3.

_____ Affiliation
_____ Achievement
_____ Power

Why do you believe this?

_____

_____

_____

_____

2

As Maslow's and McClelland's theories suggest, we work for a complex variety of reasons beyond financial compensation. Employers can encourage employee motivation by recognizing their needs and providing ways to meet them.

Employers can encourage employee motivation by recognizing their needs and providing ways to meet them.

How Much Power Does Money Have?

As we have seen, people work to fill a variety of needs, both material and psychological. Money can certainly help us meet a number of these needs, but how does it affect our motivation? Perhaps not as dramatically as we might think. In his research, theorist Frederick Herzberg found that increased money did not necessarily lead to increased worker motivation. It did, however, reduce the level of employee complaints.

> **While some employees may place a high value on money, many others do not.**

As you determine the role money will play in your workplace, consider that while some of your employees may place a high value on money, many others do not for a variety of reasons, including:

♦ They may not need much money. A single worker whose home is paid off and who makes a car last 120,000 miles will have far lower living expenses than someone with two new cars, a mortgage, and children in day care. An employee without pressing financial needs might value time off or public recognition more than money.

♦ They value other factors more than money. Some people place a greater emphasis on other factors, such as integrity, values, personal expression, or intellectual challenge. A vegetarian wouldn't work in a meat-processing plant, no matter what the salary, and a dancer would be dissatisfied with a desk job, even if it meant a substantial raise.

Even those workers who do place a substantial value on money are beginning to question their priorities. As Timothy Miller points out in his book *How to Want What You Have,* these people are beginning to realize that constantly striving for more money and the things it will buy will not bring satisfaction because:

♦ Gaining more does not eliminate sorrow, humiliation, pain, or death.

♦ Desiring more often does harm.

♦ Striving for more is not always enjoyable.

♦ Desiring more ignores spiritual longing.

As more people question their desire for money, managers will need to use other aspects of the work environment to inspire motivation. Rather than a pay increase, workers might wish for more challenging, less repetitive jobs and more opportunities to enjoy leisure time or care for their families.

2

Take a Moment

If you could name one thing that would most inspire your motivation to perform well in the workplace, what would it be? Money? Something else?

_____

_____

_____

Your Role as a Leader

Where money truly rates as a support for employee motivation varies with who's telling the story. A 1993 study conducted by *Industry Week* magazine found that it fell in the second slot. This survey of approximately 2,500 workers asked for the primary long-term motivator. The answers:

Having a leader with vision and values	32.6%
Getting pay raises and bonuses	27.5%
Gaining greater responsibility	20.7%
Gaining respect of peers and subordinates	16.6%
Achieving recognition from supervisor(s)	12.5%
Other	8.7%

The number one support for employee motivation seems to be the influence of the leader.

The number one support for employee motivation seems to be the influence of the leader. Clearly, workers respect a leader with vision; as a manager, your leadership plays a vital role in encouraging your employees. In our next chapter, we'll consider how you can provide strong leadership by setting goals for your employees that will clarify their roles and inspire their motivation.

Summary

People work for a variety of reasons. Our incomes provide us with the food and shelter we need to survive; however, our jobs also help us fill a number of psychological and emotional needs.

People work for a variety of reasons.

Abraham Maslow developed a model that places human needs in a hierarchy, as in this figure:

2

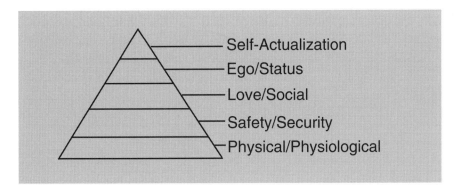

According to Maslow, as we fill our basic needs, we are able to progress up the hierarchy until we deal with concerns regarding self-fulfillment. Our jobs can help us meet many of these needs, both through the income they provide and the opportunities for social contact and challenging work.

Another model developed by David McClelland considers just those needs that are met by the workplace. These include:

1. The need for affiliation.

2. The need for achievement.

3. The need for power.

Not everyone has the same level of need for each particular area.

Money alone does not always encourage increased worker motivation.

Money can help us meet many of our needs, but money alone does not always encourage increased worker motivation. Many workers may not need much money or may value other things more. As Timothy Miller suggests, some workers are discovering that constantly striving for more money and possessions is unfulfilling.

Though money can contribute to a supportive work environment, research suggests that its influence on employee motivation is secondary compared to the vision and values of a group leader. As a manager, your leadership plays a vital role in encouraging your employees and inspiring their motivation.

Self-Check: Chapter 2 Review

Answers to these questions appear on page 108.

2

1. What are the five categories of human needs identified by Abraham Maslow?

   _____

   _____

2. How can our jobs help us meet our physical/physiological needs?

   _____

   _____

3. How can our jobs provide us with the opportunity to meet our social needs?

   _____

   _____

   _____

4. According to David McClelland, what three types of needs do people hope to satisfy specifically through work?

   _____

   _____

   _____

5. Why might some employees not value money as much as other employees?

   _____

   _____

   _____

   _____

Chapter *Three*

Establishing Your Vision

Chapter Objectives

▶ Develop a vision to inspire your department or team.

▶ Set strategic imperatives to help your team live out its vision.

▶ Measure employee progress in meeting strategic imperatives.

▶ Inspire ongoing employee motivation for Continuous Improvement.

Convey to your employees a clear vision of what you hope your organization, division, department, or team will achieve.

If the number one factor that inspires employee motivation is a manager with vision, your challenge as a manager is clear—convey to your employees a clear vision of what you hope your organization, division, department, or team will achieve. Then enable your employees to live out that vision by helping them set objectives, or *strategic imperatives*. When employees fully understand where their organization is headed and what their role is in meeting that goal, they are far more motivated than employees who are left in the dark.

Focus Your Vision

■ Joy didn't know how to react to her promotion to manager. She was excited about the pay raise and the new office, and she knew more about her department than anyone. But she doubted her leadership ability. "I just don't have charisma," she said to herself as she looked in the mirror. "How will I ever get anyone to listen to me?"

Many managers share Joy's concern. They worry that they will be unable to articulate a vision for their employees because they aren't outgoing or charismatic. But managers don't need the charm of a politician or the appeal of a movie star to inspire employee motivation. What they do need is a clear vision of what they want their department to achieve and a commitment to conveying that vision.

What Is Your Vision?

Many organizations have a vision or mission statement that describes their ultimate goals. If your organization does, you might start there and determine what your department needs to do in order to live out its part of that vision. But whether your organization has a vision statement or not, you can certainly articulate a vision for your department and convey it to your team; in fact, you should ask for your employees' input and invite them to brainstorm with you.

Your vision does not need to consider the specifics of how you will meet your goals—that comes later. What it does need to do is articulate the results you hope your department will achieve in a way that will inspire your employees. After all, if you don't have a destination in mind, how will you and your employees know when you get there?

3

Managers need a clear vision of what they want their department to achieve and a commitment to conveying that vision.

Try to sum up your vision in a single sentence. Here are a few examples, but don't let them limit your own creativity.

◆ For a research and development department: Make our organization the industry leader by generating the most innovative and best-designed products.

◆ For a word-processing department: Support management by completing all assignments on deadline, without errors.

◆ For a customer service department: Provide superior service to customers by responding to all inquiries quickly and courteously.

Take a Moment

What is your vision for your own division, department, or team? Take some time now to brainstorm. Then, try to sum up your vision in a sentence.

_____

_____

_____

_____

Set Strategic Imperatives

■ "Welcome to the firm," Carmen's new manager said enthusiastically. "Our mission at Worldwide Widgets is to become the leading widget manufacturer in the world. I know you'll work hard and do your part to make our company great."

"Thank you," Carmen answered. "I've heard a lot about the company's goals, and I think they're very exciting, but I was hoping you could tell me some specific things I can do to get started."

"Oh, I don't know; I'm not a detail person," the manager answered distractedly as she walked out the door. "Just look through the files; I'm sure you'll think of something."

3

It's hard for employees to remain inspired when they have no specific goals. Your organizational and departmental mission statements are good motivational starting points, but to maintain that motivation, you will need to set objectives, or *strategic imperatives*, for your department and your individual employees. Strategic imperatives are limited, specific goals that we can complete and measure. For example, the research and development department whose vision is to become an industry leader could set the strategic imperative of creating ten new products in the next year.

> *Strategic imperatives are limited, specific goals that we can complete and measure.*

Creating Strategic Imperatives

Each of your employees should have individual strategic imperatives that will contribute to reaching your department's overall vision. Get all of your workers involved in the process, not only in creating their own objectives, but in developing objectives for the department. Your department's overall goal should already be evident or at least outlined by you. It never hurts to remind staff members of the goal(s) if you haven't done so lately.

Work with your employees to establish strategic imperatives that are tailored to their needs. Some employees, especially those without a lot of work experience, may be intimidated by objectives that appear too difficult. They can begin with more modest strategic imperatives that will build a string of small successes before they move on to bigger objectives. Don't assign

33

any employees more strategic imperatives than they can handle. Sure, you want to get the work done, but the formidable task of trying to get a huge number of projects completed can kill motivation.

TIP: The longer a challenge has been around, the longer it will take to solve the problem. Plan accordingly when setting strategic imperatives related to such a problem so that your good workers don't get frustrated and your less-productive workers don't give up entirely.

Though you want to keep strategic imperatives manageable, leave room for those employees who are habitual overachievers. Consider the following example:

■ Gloria worked in the public relations department of a major hospital. She not only achieved those objectives set out by the marketing director but also found new areas that needed to be explored. She put in a good deal of time on her extra projects and hoped that her willingness to take on extra work would be rewarded. But, though her supervisor acknowledged her extra efforts in her performance review, there was no other reward.

Soon Gloria realized that extra work did not mean extra pay or anything else. *Why work so hard?* she thought. She began to accomplish only what was set out in her original strategic imperatives, and when she thought of new areas to tackle, she kept her mouth shut. After a few months, she decided to leave and start her own business. This wasn't part of her original career plan; she just thought it would be a good move because the traditional workplace had never valued her extra drive.

Support employees' ongoing motivation by making objectives expandable.

People who willingly take on more work, like Gloria, are hard to come by—don't lose them! Support their ongoing motivation by making their objectives expandable. Explain to employees that though there is a set list of strategic imperatives, if they see another item that needs to be included, by all means add it. Most importantly, reward them for their extra foresight and the extra work they do.

Take a Moment

Identify three employees in your department or team and write their names below. What are some strategic imperatives you could set for each employee that would help your department or team achieve its goals?

Name   **Strategic Imperatives**

_____   _____

                                  _____

_____   _____

                                  _____

_____   _____

                                  _____

_____   _____

                                  _____

3

Don't Forget the Positive

Too often, strategic imperatives are created to strengthen a weakness, as when organizations try to boost sagging sales or improve shaky customer service. Don't limit yourself to the negative. You'll be able to generate more ideas when you base some of your objectives on areas that are already successful. Plus, it's fulfilling for your staff to be reminded of the things they have done well. As you and your staff develop strategic imperatives, view your work from dual perspectives. Notice that for each element, its antithesis is included:

> **You'll be able to generate more ideas when you base some of your objectives on areas that are already successful.**

♦ What are our strengths, and how can we make them stronger?

♦ What are our weaknesses, and how can we be stronger in those areas?

♦ Who are our affiliates, and how can they help us more?

♦ Who are our competitors, and how can we compete more effectively?

♦ What outside influences threaten our productivity, and how can we lessen the impact?

♦ What outside influences boost our productivity, and how can we get more?

♦ What inside influences threaten our productivity, and how can we lessen the impact?

♦ What inside influences boost our productivity, and how can we get more?

Take a Moment

How would you answer the preceding questions? Write your responses below. Use extra paper if necessary.

_____

_____

_____

_____

_____

_____

_____

3

Measure Employee Progress

■ It was a beautiful spring afternoon, and Jerry could almost hear his favorite golf course calling his name. He knew that he was behind on his ad sales and should make some calls, but he just didn't see any point. He couldn't remember the last time anyone had actually checked his sales figures. Why should he give up this beautiful afternoon when no one would even notice?

Your employees will be much more motivated to meet their strategic imperatives if they know that their work will be recognized. That means that you will need a way to measure their productivity and achievements.

Creating Job Measures

Your job measures should relate to the type of strategic imperatives that you and an employee have agreed upon.

Job measures provide a way to quantify employees' progress in meeting their strategic imperatives. Your job measures should relate to the type of strategic imperatives that you and an employee have agreed upon. Some strategic imperatives are easier to measure than others because they deal with things that can be easily counted. If, in the previous example, Jerry had a strategic imperative to raise his sales by 20 percent, his manager could easily measure his performance. Likewise, the manager of a production worker can easily count the number of units that the worker produces in a given time period.

But some objectives are not so easy to measure. How would you measure the performance of an office manager, an accountant, or a nurse? Here are a few variables you might consider:

♦ Timeliness—Consider the number of times deadlines are met and the reasons why deadlines are missed.

♦ Accuracy—Consider the employee's ability to perform without error.

♦ Following procedures—Consider the employee's ability to follow standard procedures, such as the routine filing of reports.

Take a Moment

Think of a position in your department. What are some aspects of that position that you could measure?

_____

_____

_____

_____

_____

3

Remember that you won't be able to measure every aspect of every job—some aspects of performance are difficult to quantify. Don't give up easily, however. Look for the processes that can be measured. When you run out of ideas, think some more, read, study, ask for advice, or go to a seminar.

To help employees get the most from performance measurement, keep these guidelines in mind:

◆ Encourage staff members to see measurement as a way to promote self-growth, not as a way for you to check up on them.

◆ Communicate measurement results when it will help to do so.

◆ Make sure that you are always measuring processes, and not assessing the value of people.

◆ Measure processes related to your own position too.

Encourage staff members to see measurement as a way to promote self-growth, not as a way for you to check up on them.

39

Develop a consciousness of measurement within your organization. This will take time if it hasn't been done before. Get staff members thinking about which tasks they can measure, how they can instigate self-improvement through measures, and how they can become involved in the process of ongoing quality elevation.

TIP: Use measurement as a positive role-modeling device. Start a monthly profit review (if applicable for your organization), and each month, look for one person's effort that you can highlight. Find a specific tie-in. With some people, such as salespeople, this specific tie-in might be obvious. Vary whom you feature, however. A superstar worker can't be the focus each month, or this practice will discourage motivation in others. Remain positive. Don't use this mechanism to point out that others are doing less, aren't up to par, or aren't contributing.

Managing for Continuous Improvement

If your organization has a Continuous Improvement or Total Quality Management program in place, you will need to inspire ongoing employee motivation in order to make it effective.

> If possible, begin your quality efforts with people who already have a strong level of motivation.

If possible, begin your quality efforts with people who already have a strong level of motivation. Workers with a low level of motivation may not be ready to deal with issues of quality on an ongoing basis—if they're having trouble caring about coming to work, they will have real trouble caring about creating a quality product or service.

Work with these people in a more rudimentary way until you can understand what they need before you make a full-fledged push toward Continuous Improvement. This doesn't mean that you should ignore issues of quality completely, but rather that you should wait until some of the more basic issues are resolved before you begin discussing the fine points of Total Quality Management.

TIP: People who have difficulty maintaining their motivation over a long period of time might not be suited for an organization practicing Continuous Improvement. Total Quality Management isn't a project that starts today and is finished tomorrow—it never ends.

For those workers who already have a strong level of motivation, Continuous Improvement can be an important part of your drive to help everyone succeed. Here are some guidelines to help you support employee motivation to maintain quality.

3

◆ Emphasize that everyone is a link in the quality chain. If one link breaks, the chain breaks. Help employees recognize that quality rests not only on the shoulders of the entire group but also on the shoulders of each person.

◆ Allow each worker to overrule everyone when she or he knows something is not top quality. Quality needs to be the ultimate authority.

◆ Respect employees' judgment and give them both accountability and authority. Authority without accountability is dangerous, but together they provide the ultimate support for responsibility and motivation.

◆ Make results measurable and broadcast those results so that everyone can see progress.

◆ Make quality part of the process even when it's difficult. The test of a true quality organization is its ability to maintain high standards under pressure.

Take a Moment

Does your organization currently have a Continuous Improvement or Total Quality Management program? If so, how do workers respond to it? Can you think of anything management could do to improve employee response? List your ideas below:

_____

_____

_____

If your organization doesn't have a Continuous Improvement program in place, how do you think employees would react if one were started? What could management do to inspire employees to accept such a program?

_____

_____

_____

_____

Base Leadership in Values

You might remember that the *Industry Week* survey quoted earlier stated that employees were inspired by leaders with vision and *values*. To fully inspire, your vision for your team—and your treatment of your team members—need to be grounded in a set of values that your employees respect.

The term *values* means different things to different people. You and your employees probably do not share all the same values, nor should you expect to. However, there are some basic values shared by many people that can be particularly inspiring in the workplace. These include:

3

◆ **Respect for others**—All of your efforts to inspire motivation will be useless if you don't treat your employees with respect and set an example by treating those outside your team with consideration as well.

All of your efforts to inspire motivation will be useless if you don't treat your employees with respect.

◆ **Honesty and integrity**—As our society becomes more and more disillusioned, honesty and integrity in leadership are increasingly valued. Your employees want to know that they can trust you and that you do what you say you are going to do whether you're dealing with employees or customers.

◆ Fairness—We've all heard horror stories of the slacker who's promoted over the hardworking employee because he's the boss's friend. Though the example is exaggerated, nothing can kill motivation faster than the perception of unfairness. Avoid favoritism when dealing with employees, and be sure that your employees understand the basis for your decisions.

These are just a few of the values that can inspire motivation in your employees. Though they may seem basic, they can make the difference between employees who approach their jobs, coworkers, and customers with cynicism and those who are inspired to put forth their very best efforts. Employees who are treated with respect, honesty, and fairness will return that loyalty to their organization and reflect it when dealing with others.

Take a Moment

Are there other values that you think are important in the workplace? Add them to the list of values below, then describe actions managers can take to live out these values when dealing with employees.

Value	Action
Respect for others	_____
	_____
Honesty and integrity	_____
	_____
Fairness	_____
	_____

Maintain Your Vision

Inspiring employees' vision doesn't require personal charisma or a dynamic personality. What it does require is the ability to:

◆ Imagine the results you want your team to achieve.

◆ Identify strategic imperatives that will help your team meet those results.

◆ Determine how to measure employee progress.

◆ Maintain quality.

◆ Live out good workplace values.

Employees who understand their organization's mission and their role in meeting those goals will be better able to maintain motivation than employees who are left in the dark. In our next chapter, we'll consider how you can continue to inspire motivation by rewarding employees for a job well done.

Summary

If the number one factor that inspires employee motivation is vision, your challenge as a manager is to convey to your employees a clear vision of what you hope your department or team will achieve. You can begin to develop a team vision by examining your organization's overall vision or mission statement. Your team vision does not need to consider the specifics of how you will meet your goals, but it does need to articulate the results you hope your team will achieve in a way that will inspire your employees.

Employees are inspired by values as well as vision.

3

To remain inspired by your vision, your employees need strategic imperatives that will help them live out that vision. *Strategic imperatives* are limited, specific goals that employees can complete and measure. You should develop strategic imperatives for your department as a whole and for individual employees. Tailor imperatives for individual employees to their specific needs and involve them in the goal-setting process. As you create strategic imperatives, focus on what your department is currently doing well—as well as what needs improvement.

Maintain employee motivation to meet strategic imperatives by monitoring employee progress. Use job measures to quantify employees' progress in meeting their strategic imperatives. Some strategic imperatives are easier to measure than others because they deal with things that can be counted. Others are more difficult. To measure them, you might want to consider such variables as timelines, accuracy, and following procedures.

If your organization has a Continuous Improvement or Total Quality Management program in place, you will need to inspire ongoing employee motivation to make it effective. It's best to begin quality efforts with employees who already have a strong level of motivation—less motivated employees need more rudimentary work before they're ready for the fine points of Continuous Improvement. When you do begin quality efforts with your employees, follow these guidelines to inspire and maintain employee motivation:

◆ Emphasize that everyone is a link in the quality chain.

◆ Allow each worker to overrule everyone when she or he knows something is not top quality.

Your challenge as a manager is to convey to your employees a clear vision of what you hope your department or team will achieve.

◆ Respect employees' judgment and give them both accountability and authority.

◆ Make results measurable and broadcast those results so that everyone can see progress.

◆ Make quality part of the process even when it's difficult.

Finally, remember that employees are inspired by values as well as vision. Practicing values, such as respect for others, honesty, and fairness, will not only inspire employees, but it will also encourage them to use the same values when dealing with coworkers and customers.

Self-Check: Chapter 3 Review

Answers to these questions appear on page 108.

Answers to these questions appear on page 108.

1. What does a vision or mission statement do?

   _____

   _____

   _____

2. What are strategic imperatives?

   _____

   _____

3

3. What do job measures do?

   _____

   _____

4. Which of these is *not* a guideline for maintaining employee motivation for a quality program?

   a. Emphasize that everyone is a link in the quality chain.

   b. Allow each worker to overrule everyone when she or he knows that something is not top quality.

   c. Give employees authority, but don't hold them accountable for every decision.

   d. Make results measurable and broadcast those results so that everyone can see progress.

   e. Make quality part of the process even when it's difficult.

5. What are three values that can inspire employees?

   _____

   _____

Chapter *Four*

Rewarding Your Employees

Chapter Objectives

▶ Offer rewards that employees value.

▶ Distribute rewards fairly.

▶ Use monetary and recognition rewards effectively.

▶ Keep rewards from backfiring.

Rewards can inspire employee motivation, but only if managers match the right reward to the right worker.

What gets rewarded gets done. The statement is true, but a bit too simple. Rewards can inspire employee motivation, but only if managers match the right reward to the right worker. A poorly planned reward system may do nothing to encourage employee motivation, or at worst, may actually discourage it.

To ensure that rewards work to support motivation instead of hinder it, managers need to understand the relationship between rewards and motivation as well as the features of an effective reward system.

Inspiring Motivation Through Rewards

There are many different types of rewards. In the workplace, rewards typically include money, promotions, job titles, attractive offices, praise from the boss or peers, bonuses, and perks such as a company car.

If all rewards could inspire motivation in all employees, your job as a manager would be easy—simply offer any reward and watch motivation skyrocket. But rewards can be tricky. Sometimes they succeed in inspiring employee motivation, and sometimes they don't, as in the examples on the next page:

■ Juanita loves praise and appreciates a compliment even more than a financial reward. When she is praised by her supervisor or coworkers, she practically skips around the office! The next time she's asked to perform a certain function, she does it even more enthusiastically than before, remembering her past positive experiences.

■ Terry, on the other hand, has trouble accepting compliments. He's a dedicated worker who maintains high standards of quality. But when praised for a job well done, he's actually a little embarrassed. His inner thoughts are, "I just got lucky this time."

In our first example, praise inspired the employee motivation the manager hoped for. In our second example, though, the praise actually created a negative response—there was no support for motivation. Terry's manager would have received a better response if he had offered Terry some other type of reward, like money or extra time off. The contrast between the two employees points out the importance of creating a reward system that offers the right reward to the right worker.

4

Take a Moment

Think of those you supervise. Can you identify which types of rewards are is most likely to inspire a positive response? List them below. Keep in mind that few people, if any, are motivated solely by one type of reward. Look for which of the two types is predominant.

Name	Reward Type
_____	_____
_____	_____
_____	_____
_____	_____
_____	_____

Choose Rewards Carefully

As we saw in the previous example, there is no guarantee that the reward you offer will inspire motivation. However, there are some things you can do to make it more likely that your employees will react favorably to the rewards you offer. Generally, employees are more likely to react favorably to a reward if:

◆ The employee values the reward and sees the reward as worth the effort it will take to earn it.

◆ The employee understands how to earn the reward; the reward is clearly linked to specific behaviors.

◆ The employee sees the reward as attainable; the performance level necessary is reachable.

◆ The employee sees the reward system as fair.

Offer a Reward the Employee Values

Case Study

■ "If we increase our productivity by 20 percent this quarter, you'll all get a great reward!" Bartholomew announced to his staff. "Can't tell you what it is yet—it's a surprise!"

Dreaming of a sizable cash bonus that would pay off her credit cards, Miranda worked hard. During breaks, she and other staff members gossiped about what the reward might be. But after a few days, the excited chatter in the break room turned sour.

"I want to know what the reward is," Miranda's friend Minh Lo complained. "I've never worked so hard in my life, and all we might be getting is a nickel-an-hour raise."

The complaints got so bad that Bartholomew finally revealed the reward: If the productivity goal was met, each department member would get a free cruise! The plant would have down time in June while new equipment was being installed. The whole department could go together on a one-week vacation to sunny shores! All expenses were paid, but the staff would have to use their own vacation days.

Miranda immediately lost her motivation to meet the goal. Why?

1. She didn't like boats or water.

2. She was a single mother of twin preschool boys. Getting a baby-sitter would be tough, and she didn't want to leave her children for a full week.

3. She sure as heck didn't want to spend her vacation time with her coworkers!

In the following weeks, Miranda learned that several of her coworkers had similar reactions. She wasn't surprised when the quarterly production goals weren't met.

4

Though Miranda wasn't surprised when production goals weren't met, her supervisor undoubtedly was. But Bartholomew should never have assumed that all of his staff members would place the same value on his offer.

As this example illustrates, people's reactions to rewards vary according to their life circumstances and individual preferences. When employees don't value a reward, they won't be motivated to make the effort to earn it. Instead of offering an incentive to his staff without knowing their preferences, Bartholomew should have done some homework to learn what types of rewards his employees did value.

> **People's reactions to rewards vary according to their life circumstances and individual preferences.**

Though employees shouldn't dictate every aspect of a reward system, you should certainly take their needs and desires into account. You can develop some understanding of their preferences simply by visiting with them in the break room or other informal settings. You can also learn about them through more formal situations, such as performance appraisals or departmental meetings. You might even consider asking employees to fill out a survey, such as the one on the next page.

Take a Moment

I would like (check one of the three):

Job Element	More	Less	Currently okay
Praise	_____	_____	_____
Supervision	_____	_____	_____
Direction	_____	_____	_____
Being on a team	_____	_____	_____
Leading a team	_____	_____	_____
Goals	_____	_____	_____
Structure	_____	_____	_____
Chance for promotion	_____	_____	_____
Chance for education/training	_____	_____	_____
Flexibility of workplace	_____	_____	_____
Flexibility of work time	_____	_____	_____
Decision making	_____	_____	_____
Workload	_____	_____	_____
Meetings	_____	_____	_____
Responsibility	_____	_____	_____
Recognition	_____	_____	_____

Take a Moment *(continued)*

I would like (check one of the three):

Job Element	More	Less	Currently okay
Respect	_____	_____	_____
Freedom of expression	_____	_____	_____
Awards	_____	_____	_____
Salary	_____	_____	_____
Vacation	_____	_____	_____
Personal days	_____	_____	_____
Cash value of medical/dental benefits, insurance, etc.	_____	_____	_____
Cash bonus	_____	_____	_____

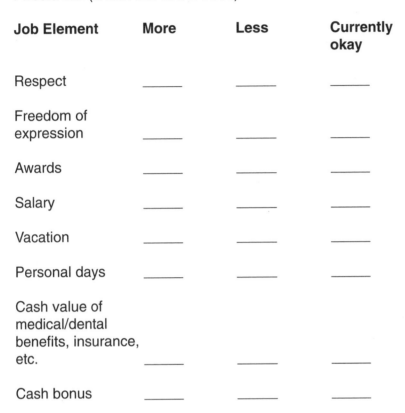

4

You may not be able to give your employees some of these items at this time. Keep them on the list anyway. If you find an astounding result, such as the fact that your entire staff wants more personal days, perhaps you can begin to change the company structure so that eventually you can provide them.

You might try giving employees two copies of the survey. Ask them to fill out one copy to reflect what they would like to receive from you, and complete the other to reflect what they would like to receive from their peers. Items such as "salary" that cannot be provided by peers could be designated N/A (not applicable).

Clearly Explain How to Earn the Reward

■ Ivan had worked at Happy Burger for two years, and he'd never been named Employee of the Month. All of his coworkers had seen their photos posted on the special Employee of the Month bulletin board and been allowed to park in the special Employee of the Month parking space, but he was always left out. Finally, he decided to ask his supervisor.

"I've always wondered why I've never been named Employee of the Month," Ivan said to his supervisor one afternoon. "Could you tell me what I'd have to do to be considered?"

"Work a lot harder than you do now, that's what," the supervisor said with a laugh.

A reward won't inspire an employee if the employee doesn't know how to earn it.

A reward won't inspire an employee if the employee doesn't know how to earn it. As a manager, you must establish the performance level to be achieved in a specific way. Simply telling someone to "do better" isn't good enough; a staff member must have a clearer goal.

If you have difficulty setting specific goals for your employees, review the previous chapter, especially the section on job measures. Some achievements can be difficult to measure numerically, but even if you can't translate a task into numbers, it is possible to get specific. For example, Ivan's supervisor at Happy Burger might have talked about whether Ivan arrived at work on time, was polite to customers, and was able to fill orders without errors.

Be Sure That the Reward Is Attainable

■ At Keisha's advertising agency, account executives were rewarded financially for bringing in new accounts. Though Keisha was swamped with work on her existing accounts, she needed cash for a new home. Her supervisor told her that she'd get a 10 percent commission on the first-year client billings if she could bring in at least a $500,000 annual-budget account.

Excited at the thought of moving into her new home, Keisha began to think about the process of gaining a new account of that size. Sure, she could have assistance from some of the creative staff to put interesting ideas together for client pitches. But after talking with others and reviewing the small pool of businesses from which to draw, Keisha realized that getting such a sizable account was a Herculean task. Besides, where would she get the time? She'd literally have to work 24 hours a day to serve all of her regular clients and develop a winning presentation. Keisha finally gave up, deciding that she didn't have the ability to get such a large account anyway.

This attempt to inspire motivation suffered because the employee didn't perceive the reward as being attainable. The belief that one has at least a chance of reaching the performance level required to earn a reward is central to that reward's ability to inspire motivation. As Keisha's story illustrates, an unattainable reward can turn against itself. Staff members can become bitter or resentful when they perceive a reward as impossible to achieve; eventually, they may begin to doubt their overall abilities.

> An un-attainable reward can turn against itself.

Managers walk a fine line in determining the level of performance to be rewarded. On one hand, the goal must be high enough to present a challenge to the employee, or else the reward will be meaningless. On the other hand, the performance level cannot be so high that the employee sees it as unreasonable or impossible.

In Keisha's case, her boss knew that the agency would profit if Keisha could land a huge client. But the boss gave little thought to Keisha's actual ability to do it given her time and resource constraints. Instead, the boss thought, "Why not offer that carrot on a stick? If Keisha can't achieve it, we have nothing to lose." But the agency had something BIG to lose—Keisha's motivation.

55

Take a Moment

Has there been a time when you wanted a particular reward and couldn't get it? How did it affect you? Jot down your thoughts below. If you haven't experienced this personally (and that puts you in a fortunate minority), then think about a similar situation involving someone you know—how did it affect that person?

Reward:

_____

_____

Performance required to get the reward:

_____

_____

Personal belief level that the award could be earned:
0 = No belief; 10 = Total confidence
Circle one:

1   2   3   4   5   6   7   8   9   10

What happened:

_____

_____

_____

_____

_____

_____

Establish a Fair Reward System

■ Greta tore eagerly at her pay envelope. Her bonus check was inside. Steve had bragged all month about the new stereo system he'd bought with his last bonus. She knew she'd sold just as much as he had, and she had plenty of uses for the money. But when she saw the amount of her check, her anticipation changed to anger. This check couldn't be anywhere near what Steve had gotten—why was there such a difference?

"I wonder if it's because I'm a woman?" Greta asked herself. If that was the case, what was the use of putting out her best effort? No matter what she did, she'd never get ahead.

To inspire motivation in all your employees, your reward system must be equitable. If Steve gets a $500 bonus for reaching a sales quota, and Greta gets $250 for reaching the same quota, this spells trouble (and in this case, possible charges of discrimination). Though this point might seem obvious, remember that reward systems can become skewed because of the supervisor's perception of various employees.

4

> **To inspire motivation in all your employees, your reward system must be equitable.**

Suppose that you set up a bonus structure to reward your employees for reaching their sales goals. You felt certain that your cooperative, friendly employees—José, Sandra, and Bill—would achieve it. But Ryan, who is on probation for tardiness, and who you suspect has a drinking problem, achieves the goal first. Would you be tempted to give Ryan less than the others because he's on probation? Some supervisors would. But ask yourself what this would do to the equity of the reward system—and to Ryan's motivation. If there's no consistency in your rewards, the whole system could fall apart.

Following these guidelines will help you establish an effective reward system for your employees. Next, we'll consider how to use two of the most common types of rewards: money and recognition.

Take a Moment

Review the last reward that you offered your employees. Did it follow all four of the guidelines we just discussed? Check them off on the list below:

_____ The employee values the reward and sees the reward as worth the effort it will take to earn it.

_____ The employee understands how to earn the reward; the reward is clearly linked to specific behaviors.

_____ The employee sees the reward as attainable; the performance level necessary is reachable.

_____ The employee sees the reward system as fair.

Did your reward system work? Why or why not? If you didn't follow all of the guidelines, list the ones you missed and how leaving them out affected the plan.

_____

_____

_____

_____

_____

Use Monetary Rewards and Recognition Effectively

Managers reward employees in hundreds, if not thousands, of ways. Two of the most basic types of rewards are:

◆ Monetary rewards that offer a financial incentive for good performance.

◆ Recognition rewards that show appreciation for good performance.

Rewarding with Money

As we saw in Chapter 2, people's reactions to money vary so greatly that you shouldn't rely on it as your sole support for employee motivation. Money does, however, have its place in the supportive work environment. When you do use money to inspire employee motivation, use it most effectively by keeping the following guidelines in mind:

◆ **Workers must see a correlation between good work and higher earnings.** Anything else skews their sense of reality. Imagine paying the office slacker a higher salary than the top-performing manager. No one would know what to expect in such a convoluted system, and soon, no one would care.

◆ **Workers must see that compensation varies according to various levels of performance.** Giving everyone a 5 percent raise and no other incentive will not encourage employee motivation. Many organizations employ a more complex system, providing cost-of-living increases, rewards for company-wide performance (a universal, equal reward), rewards for departmental performance (an equal reward for members of a particular group), and rewards for individual performance (a reward customized for an individual). This mix encourages a variety of positive behaviors related to both individual achievement and teamwork.

◆ **Workers ought to have a general idea of salary levels but not specific individual information.** In days past, secrecy about others' pay was paramount. This clandestine approach tempts individual workers to believe that everyone else makes much more money than they do. But if an employee

4

Workers
must see a
correlation
between good
work and higher
earnings.

knows that he or she is on "level 16" and that supervisors typically are on "level 18," the employee can realistically estimate the difference in salary ranges.

Conversely, though, discovering specific information about another individual's pay level or bonus can discourage motivation. A disliked manager who is highly productive will be even more disliked if others find out he got a 17 percent raise when everybody else got 8 percent or less. A hardworking 25-year-old might like her 50-year-old coworker until she discovers that by seniority alone the older worker makes double her salary.

Discovering specific information about another individual's pay level or bonus can discourage motivation.

TIP: A clever monetary reward is to give a cash bonus numerically equal to company profits. For instance (if this wouldn't destroy your company's budget), each person could get a $500 bonus because the company made an extra $500,000 gross in a given year. Or, if company profits rose 14 percent, each employee could get a cash bonus equal to 14 percent of their salary. Evaluate all possibilities before you make such an offer. If your employees are striving to reach that goal, and your business waxes and wanes dramatically because of the whims of suppliers, it won't help much to set up this system.

Take a Moment

Does your organization currently follow the guidelines for effectively using monetary rewards listed previously? If not, what are some ways your organization could begin to improve its use of money to inspire motivation? List them below:

_____

_____

_____

_____

_____

Rewarding with Recognition

There are many types of rewards that do not involve money or other material incentives, such as a bigger office or a company car. Recognition rewards can inspire motivation by showing employees that their hard work is noticed and appreciated. Some common types of recognition rewards include:

◆ **Giving an employee more responsibility and decision-making authority**. You don't need to give an employee a formal promotion to empower that person with more responsibility and authority. Many workers crave more control over their own work projects and would enjoy the chance to serve as a team facilitator or group leader. Identify those employees and give them the chance to grow—and be sure that they understand that with responsibility comes accountability.

TIP: Giving someone added responsibility does not mean just throwing more work at them. Be sure that your assignments are reasonable and that the employee will find the new responsibility truly challenging instead of more of the same old routine.

◆ **Recognizing an employee publicly**. Many employees enjoy having their achievements recognized publicly. The acknowledgment can be as simple as briefly mentioning the employee's accomplishment during a staff meeting:

■ "We'd like to congratulate Monique for making $45,000 in sales last month. That's a personal best for her."

Or your efforts can be more involved, such as giving the employee a plaque or taking the employee to lunch.

TIP: Some employees are shy or come from cultures in which public recognition is not considered appropriate. Get to know the members of your team and their preferences regarding public recognition. If you are unsure, ASK. And if an employee doesn't care for public recognition, don't forget to acknowledge her or his achievements privately.

> Recognition rewards can inspire motivation by showing employees that their hard work is noticed and appreciated.

4

◆ **Instituting a formal recognition program.** Reward outstanding achievement by starting a formal reward program that recognizes outstanding achievement on a regular basis. Many organizations have Employee of the Month programs; you might consider starting something similar for your department or team.

TIP: If you do institute a formal recognition program, be sure that all employees understand the level of performance necessary to be recognized, and stress that all employees are capable of achieving it. Keep an eye out for employee successes so that you will be able to vary the individuals recognized—recognizing the same two or three people month after month can discourage the motivation of the other employees.

> Don't wait for a performance evaluation to tell your employees they're doing a good job.

◆ **Praising an employee informally.** Don't wait for a performance evaluation to tell your employees they're doing a good job—look for good performance and praise it regularly. Use praise to build morale and support motivation by following these guidelines:

- *Focus praise on performance, not personal qualities.* You may have many different reactions to the appearance and personality of your individual employees. But your role as a manager is to focus on their actions when performing their jobs. Rather than complimenting Flora on her attractiveness, praise her ability to handle customer requests quickly and efficiently.

- *Make praise authentic.* Don't give praise unless you truly mean it, but when you see performance that deserves praise, be sure to give it.

- *Ensure that praise comes often enough to keep up morale, but not so often that it is expected.* This is a tough call. If someone is performing especially well, do you slow down your praise because you feel you're giving too many compliments too often? Not if your praise is authentic. Just don't make your praise a rigid routine, such as one compliment per day, per employee. If employees realize that they're receiving the Compliment du Jour, the praise won't have as much inherent value.

- *Understand how praise affects each individual that you supervise.* Some people enjoy receiving praise so much that they prefer it over a financial reward; some people are so shy that they are embarrassed even by private praise. Some people value other recognition, such as increased decision-making power and responsibility, more than praise. Identify people for whom praise is not effective. Look for other types of recognition that can inspire motivation.

4

Take a Moment

Are you using praise as effectively as you could? Write "yes" or "no" next to the following guidelines:

Do you . . .

_____	Give praise when it's deserved?
_____	Make certain that praise is authentic?
_____	Ensure that praise comes often enough to keep up morale but not so often that it is expected?
_____	Understand how praise affects each individual you supervise?

Based on your answers, what could you do to make your use of praise more effective?

_____

_____

_____

_____

_____

Don't Let Rewards Backfire

Some rewards can have negative as well as positive consequences.

As you decide what rewards to offer your employees, keep in mind that some rewards can have negative as well as positive consequences. When you reward the achievement of some employees with bonuses, public recognition, a nice office, or a reserved parking space, you run the risk of alienating employees who believe that they, too, should be rewarded.

Though there is no way to totally eliminate feelings of jealousy on the part of your employees, you can reduce that negative emotion by following these simple guidelines.

◆ **Be as fair as possible in your distribution of rewards.** Be sure that those singled out for rewards fully deserve them. Most employees recognize a hard worker and will not resent that person being rewarded.

◆ **Monitor employee performance and recognize hard work on the part of all employees.** Most employees will not resent the recognition of others if their work is recognized too. This does not mean that you must give every employee a sizable bonus on a regular basis, but it does mean that you should acknowledge their successes as often as possible.

◆ **Find ways to recognize smaller accomplishments as well as larger ones.** Not everyone will earn the Salesperson of the Year award. How can you recognize those who work consistently with good results?

◆ **Set reasonable performance standards for rewards, and regularly let all employees know how they can reach them.** Employees who believe that their own work is appreciated and that they have a chance to meet performance standards will be much more likely to celebrate other employees' accomplishments instead of resenting them.

Take a Moment

Is your organization doing all it can to distribute rewards fairly? Using the guidelines from the previous page, identify ways in which your organization deals effectively with rewards and areas in which it could use improvement.

Effective Use of Rewards

_____

_____

_____

_____

Areas That Need Improvement

_____

_____

_____

_____

4

Reward Good Performance

Rewarding your employees' good performance lets them know that you notice their efforts and appreciate them, which can inspire motivation. But rewards are not the only means of inspiring employee motivation. In our next chapter, we'll consider how maintaining a positive work environment can also support and encourage motivation.

Summary

Rewards can inspire employee motivation, but only if managers match the right reward to the right worker. Generally, employees are more likely to react favorably to a reward if:

♦ The employee values the reward and sees the reward as worth the effort it will take to earn it.

♦ The employee understands how to earn the reward; the reward is clearly linked to specific behaviors.

♦ The employee sees the reward as attainable; the performance level necessary is reachable.

♦ The employee sees the reward system as fair.

Two of the most basic ways that employers reward employees are with:

♦ Monetary rewards that offer a financial incentive for good performance.

♦ Recognition rewards that show appreciation for good performance.

Monetary rewards have the most beneficial influence on employee motivation when:

♦ Employees have some control over their performance.

♦ Employees can see a correlation between good work and higher earnings.

♦ Employees can see a salary spread between various levels of performance.

♦ Employees have a general ideal of salary levels but not specific individual information.

Recognition rewards can inspire motivation by showing employees that their hard work is noticed and appreciated. Some common types of recognition rewards include:

◆ Giving an employee more responsibility and decision-making authority.

◆ Recognizing an employee publicly.

◆ Instituting a formal recognition program.

◆ Praising an employee informally.

Your praise of an employee's performance will be most effective if you:

◆ Focus praise on performance, not personal qualities.

◆ Make praise authentic.

◆ Ensure that praise comes often enough to keep up morale, but not so often that it is expected.

◆ Understand how praise affects each individual whom you supervise.

Whenever you single out some employees for rewards, you run the risk that other employees will be jealous. Though there is no way to totally eliminate feelings of jealousy on the part of your employees, you can reduce that negative emotion by following these simple guidelines.

◆ Be as fair as possible in your distribution of rewards.

◆ Monitor employee performance and recognize hard work on the part of all employees.

◆ Find ways to recognize smaller accomplishments as well as larger ones.

◆ Set reasonable performance standards for rewards, and regularly let all employees know how they can reach them.

Use rewards to let your employees know that you notice and appreciate their hard work.

Self-Check: Chapter 4 Review

Answers to these questions appear on page 109.

1. True or False?
   A reward can be effective even if an employee doesn't value what is being offered.

2. True or False?
   A reward can be effective only if an employee sees it as attainable.

3. Which of the following is *not* a guideline for using money to inspire employee motivation?
   a. Workers need some control over their performance.
   b. Workers must see a correlation between good work and higher earnings.
   c. Workers should see that compensation varies according to level of performance.
   d. Workers should have specific information about the salaries of coworkers and managers.

4. True or False?
   Praising employees is important. If you can't find anything to praise about their performance, compliment them on their appearance.

5. List four things you can do to keep rewards from backfiring.

   a. _____

   b. _____

   c. _____

   d. _____

Chapter*Five*

Maintaining a Positive Work Environment

Chapter Objectives

▶ Recognize positive reinforcement, negative reinforcement, and punishment.

▶ Rely on positive rather than negative reinforcement.

▶ Create a friendly company culture.

With the exception of the independently wealthy, most of us have to work in order to survive. But as we saw in Chapter 2, we also work because we want to. We find that many of our emotional and psychological needs are filled through our work, and we enjoy our jobs.

Create a work environment in which employees feel respected and empowered.

As a manager, you can help employees want to come to work and help support employee motivation by creating a work environment in which employees feel respected and empowered. Two techniques that can help you create this type of positive work environment include:

◆ Emphasizing positive reinforcement.

◆ Creating a friendly corporate culture.

Emphasize Positive Reinforcement

Many of our ideas about reinforcement come from the work of
B. F. Skinner. Skinner studied the ways in which animal
behavior could be influenced by reinforcement. He identified
three basic types of reinforcement:

◆ Positive reinforcement

◆ Negative reinforcement

◆ Punishment

These types of reinforcement have numerous applications to
human behavior and are often used by managers in the
workplace.

◆ Managers give positive reinforcement when they reward
positive employee behavior with a positive response. The
positive response may take many forms, such as praise,
public recognition, or a monetary reward. A manager
might offer positive reinforcement by saying something
like, *"If you meet the new production quota, you'll get a bonus."*

◆ Managers give negative reinforcement when they reward
positive employee behavior by not carrying through on a
negative response. This type of reinforcement is similar to a
threat; the negative response may be fairly serious, such as a
lost job or demotion, or relatively minor, such as a wrist-
slapping from the boss. A manager might offer negative
reinforcement by saying something like, *"If you don't meet
your production quota, you'll lose your job."* By meeting the
quota, the employee avoids the negative consequence of
being fired.

◆ Managers use punishment when they meet negative behavior
with a negative response. As with the other types of
reinforcement, the punishment may take many forms, with
varying degrees of severity. A manager might offer
punishment by saying something like, *"You didn't meet your
production quota, so I'm docking your salary."*

5

71

Take a Moment

Identify which statements are examples of positive reinforcement (PR), negative reinforcement (NR), and punishment (P). Answers are given on page 109.

___1. "Those boxes need to be loaded on the truck in the next hour, or you'll have some explaining to do."

___2. "I want to recognize Jacqueline for the wonderful job she did preparing the bid for the Garland contract. Because of her hard work, we got the job."

___3. "Randy, your sales figures are low for the third time this month. I'm putting you on probation."

___4. "If you make this many typing errors on your next assignment, I'll have to put a note in your personnel file."

Negative reinforcement and punishment can build a workplace climate of fear and distrust.

If you've been a manager for any length of time, you've probably used negative reinforcement and punishment on at least a few occasions. Use of negative reinforcement can be especially tempting because threats of reduced salaries or job loss can lead to improved employee performance in the short term. But in the long run, repeated use of negative reinforcement and punishment can build a workplace climate of fear and distrust in which workers feel that their job security is constantly threatened. Such feelings are bound to discourage employee motivation.

(Note that while punishment is not an effective means of *encouraging* employee performance either, there may be times when you will need to discipline employees who have broken organizational rules, such as employees who are habitually late or who harass other employees. When this occurs, use your organization's official disciplinary channels.)

Supporting good performance through positive reinforcement is a more effective way of letting employees know the level of job performance you expect. Even an employee who is having trouble on the job must have one or two small successes. Point these out and talk with the employee about how she or he can extend the same level of performance to other aspects of the job.

Take a Moment

To examine just how damaging negative reinforcement is, think back on your own early experiences with negative reinforcement.

1. What is your first memory of negative reinforcement?

_____

_____

   Did it work? Why or why not?

_____

_____

2. How did it make you feel about the person issuing the demand? _____

_____

_____

3. What was your worst school-age experience with negative reinforcement? _____

_____

_____

4. Which teachers motivated with negative reinforcement, and what threats did they use? _____

_____

_____

_____

5

Take a Moment *(continued)*

5. What work experiences have you had with negative reinforcement, and how did they affect you?

_____

_____

6. Have you used negative reinforcement when dealing with employees? What was the cause—anger, impatience, inability to think of another approach?

_____

_____

7. What were the short-term and long-term effects of negative reinforcement? (Be honest when answering this last question. Temporary improvements in job performance can mask feelings of resentment, distrust, and fear created by negative reinforcement.) Do you know how your employees really feel?

_____

_____

_____

> The only way you can learn what type of positive reinforcement to offer your employees is to get to know them as individuals.

Choose the Right Positive Reinforcement

Knowing which type of reward to offer to which employee is an important part of using positive reinforcement effectively. We've already seen that individual employees can react quite differently to praise, public recognition, and monetary rewards. The only way you can learn what type of positive reinforcement to offer your employees is to get to know them as individuals. Then you can reinforce from a position of strength rather than guessing wildly. Plus, getting to know your employees usually means spending more time with them, which in itself is a form of positive reinforcement.

One word of caution: As you get acquainted with your employees, don't become so carried away that your efforts start to resemble a full-scale investigation into their private lives. Your job as a manager is to discover your employees' professional goals and to learn what rewards inspire motivation and good performance—not to pry into personal issues.

Create a Friendly Organizational Culture

Besides positively reinforcing employees on an individual level, you can also build goodwill at the group level by creating an organizational culture that's friendly to employees. A worker-friendly organization can inspire both motivation and organizational loyalty.

> A worker-friendly organization can inspire both motivation and organizational loyalty.

Every organization has its own unique culture. Some start-up software companies, for example, pride themselves on being young and innovative. Their employees dress in casual clothes and develop computer programs that utilize the latest technology. Employees are encouraged to "think outside the lines" and take risks so that these companies stay on the cutting edge of software design. Insurance companies, on the other hand, often present a more conservative image. Their employees might wear business suits five days a week and search for investments that are secure rather than innovative.

Your organization's culture might match one of these personae—or it might fit somewhere in between. But however you characterize your organizational culture, there are things you and other managers can do to make that culture friendly toward employees, including:

◆ Offering opportunities for education and training.

◆ Offering flexibility to deal with family issues.

◆ Respecting the diversity of your workforce.

◆ Accommodating physically challenged employees.

◆ Providing opportunities to socialize outside work.

5

Offer Opportunities for Education and Training

Nothing can discourage motivation quicker than being told to complete a task you have no idea how to perform. This type of situation has become increasingly common as the workplace becomes more technologically advanced. How many employees have found computers sitting on their desks that they have no idea how to use?

When your organization offers training to employees, it tells employees that it values them and wants to make an investment in their future. Employees who feel confident in their skills will enjoy their work more and become greater assets to their organization.

Offering training to employees tells workers that your organization values them and wants to make an investment in their future.

Offer Flexibility to Deal with Family Issues

It's hard to concentrate on a job when you have a sick child at home or an aging parent facing surgery. Many businesses are finding creative ways to help employees deal with family responsibilities and emergencies. Some alternatives you might consider include:

♦ Offering flex-time so that parents can divide child-care duties.

♦ Offering on-site day care so that parents can work near their children.

♦ Allowing employees to work at home occasionally so that they can be near sick relatives.

♦ Providing employees with personal days to deal with family issues.

Giving your employees the flexibility to deal with family issues can help reduce employee turnover.

Giving your employees the flexibility to deal with family issues can help reduce employee turnover. It also shows employees that your organization cares about them as human beings as well as workers.

Take a Moment

What are some things your organization currently does to help employees meet the needs of their families?

_____

_____

What other things could your organization offer to help employees meet family needs?

_____

_____

_____

Respect the Diversity of Your Workforce

As American society becomes increasingly diverse, that diversity is reflected in the workplace. Now, more than ever before, people from a variety of different ethnic groups, faiths, and socioeconomic backgrounds are asked to work together.

Employees from diverse backgrounds appreciate an employer who respects their diversity and expects all members of the organization to do the same. Be sure that all of your employees understand that harassment and discrimination will not be tolerated in your workplace. Remind employees that they may not all share the same religious holidays, and give them the opportunity to get to know and appreciate aspects of each other's cultures.

Accommodate Physically Challenged Employees

Accommodating physically challenged employees isn't just a nice thing to do—under the Americans with Disabilities Act, it's the law. Help your organization do whatever it can to adapt to the needs of the differently abled, and help all employees judge coworkers on the basis of their abilities, not their disabilities.

5

> Employees from diverse backgrounds appreciate an employer who respects their diversity.

Provide Opportunities to Socialize

Work is more enjoyable when you like the people you work with. Your chance of liking them increases with the amount of social time you spend together.

There are many ways to get employees together outside the workplace besides the annual company barbecue. Regular group outings at sports and entertainment events (with free or discounted tickets), discounted employee memberships at a nearby health club (or better yet, company-paid memberships), and impromptu get-togethers after work are just a few ways you can unify people and help them to enjoy the company more.

You can also build small social gatherings into the workday—special lunches, on-site parties, etc. All corporate-culture activities should be handled carefully so that they are appropriate, legal, and inclusive.

Be creative as you think of ways to brighten your corporate culture. One innovative advertising agency even produced an annual yearbook with pictures of all the staff. Just as in high school, employees took time off when the yearbooks came out to chat and collect each other's signatures!

To develop more ideas for organizational social opportunities, list the following:

◆ Activities your organization currently conducts

◆ Social activities you've enjoyed with coworkers in past jobs

◆ People who would be good at managing extracurricular corporate activities

◆ Costs involved in launching new activities

Don't work in a vacuum. Invite employees from across the organization to share their ideas for social activities. Sharing those ideas could become a social activity in itself.

Take a Moment

Brainstorm some initial ideas for opportunities for
organizational social events.

Activities we currently have in place:

_____

_____

_____

_____

_____

_____

New events we could try:

_____

_____

_____

_____

_____

_____

5

Creating a Positive Work Environment

Positive reinforcement and a worker-friendly corporate culture
are two factors that can create a positive work environment.
When a work environment is pleasant, employees will enjoy
coming to work, and they will be motivated to do their best.
They will also feel loyalty to their organization, which will result
in less employee turnover.

Summary

As a manager, you can help employees want to come to work and help support employee motivation by creating a work environment in which employees feel respected and empowered. Two techniques that can help you create this type of positive work environment include:

◆ Emphasizing positive reinforcement.

◆ Creating a friendly corporate culture.

Many of our ideas about reinforcement come from the work of B. F. Skinner. He identified three basic types of reinforcement:

◆ **Positive reinforcement**—rewarding positive behavior with a positive response: *"If you meet the new production quota, you'll get a bonus."*

◆ **Negative reinforcement**—rewarding positive behavior by not carrying through on a negative response: *"If you don't meet your production quota, you'll lose your job."*

◆ **Punishment**—meeting negative behavior with a negative response: *"You didn't meet your production quota, so I'm docking your salary."*

Though negative reinforcement may encourage improved employee performance in the short run, in the long term, both negative reinforcement and punishment can discourage employee motivation by creating a workplace climate of fear and mistrust. Positive reinforcement is a more effective way of letting employees know your expectations because it creates a positive workplace that supports employee motivation.

Because individual employees react differently to various types of positive reinforcement, managers need to get to know their employees and their individual preferences in order to offer the right type of reinforcement to the right employee.

Creating an organizational culture that is friendly toward employees will also encourage strong motivation. Some ways you can do this include:

♦ Offering opportunities for education and training.

♦ Offering flexibility to deal with family issues.

♦ Respecting the diversity of your workforce.

♦ Accommodating physically challenged employees.

♦ Providing opportunities to socialize outside work.

5

Self-Check: Chapter 5 Review

Answers to these questions appear on page 109.

1. Match the following terms to the appropriate definition.
   ____ Positive reinforcement
   ____ Negative reinforcement
   ____ Punishment
       a. Rewarding positive behavior by not carrying through on a negative response
       b. Meeting negative behavior with a negative response
       c. Rewarding positive behavior with a positive response

2. How do negative reinforcement and punishment discourage employee motivation?

   _____

   _____

   _____

3. Individual employees react differently to different types of positive reinforcement. How can managers match the right positive reinforcement to the right employee?

   _____

   _____

   _____

4. Which of the following is *not* a technique that employers can use to create an organizational culture that is friendly to employees?
   a. Offering opportunities for education and training
   b. Encouraging employees to ignore family issues
   c. Respecting the diversity of your workforce

5. Your chance of liking your fellow employees increases with

_____.

Chapter *Six*

Maintaining Open Communication

Chapter Objectives

▶ Communicate regularly and appropriately with employees.

▶ Visit employees in their work areas.

▶ Actively listen to employee concerns.

▶ Accept constructive feedback from employees.

Case Study

Today's employees want to know where their organization is headed and have the chance to share their ideas and opinions. How important is communication in supporting employee motivation? Consider the following case study:

■ Since his company's downsizing, Blaine had been busier than ever—too busy to spend time visiting with his employees. When he arrived in the morning, he greeted whomever he happened to see, and he spoke to the rest at the weekly staff meeting. He was just too stressed to deal with anything more.

Blaine didn't realize how his lack of communication affected his staff until his assistant, Max, asked to meet with him. The staff was beginning to wonder what was wrong, Max explained. The only time most of them saw Blaine anymore was at the weekly meeting, where he spent most of his time telling them that they needed to work harder. When employees tried to bring up issues of their own, Blaine interrupted, squelching their ideas. The staff was afraid that another round of layoffs was in the works.

Blaine had noticed that his department's productivity was falling off, but he'd attributed it to the increased workload. Now he was beginning to wonder if there could be another reason . . . .

In a different department, Isabella tried to remain positive. Though the recent layoffs had created some extra challenges for her, she always tried to bring out the best in her staff.

"How do you do it?" one of her staff members asked. "Even in our craziest times, you manage to stay positive. We know this project is hard, but we always look forward to your comments because they're so helpful. Because of you, we're proud of ourselves!"

Isabella was thrilled to hear that comment. It took extra energy to take care of her staff when she was feeling stressed, but Isabella knew that if she supported her people, they'd support her.

Maintaining open communication with your employees helps inspire motivation.

Maintaining open communication with your employees helps inspire and maintain their motivation. But open communication means more than just a hurried staff meeting or a quick "good morning" as you walk in the door. Truly open communication involves a number of factors, including:

6

◆ Communicating regularly with employees in ways that meet their needs.

◆ Visiting employees in their work areas.

◆ Listening to employee concerns.

◆ Accepting constructive feedback from employees.

Communicate Regularly— and Appropriately

"I don't know, I just work here." This may be the punchline to an old joke, but it's also the way many employees feel about their organizations—they simply don't know what's going on. When employees feel uninformed and ignored, they often believe that their contribution to the organization isn't valued, which discourages their motivation. You can support strong motivation by communicating regularly with your employees and by adapting your communication to meet their needs.

Communication in today's workplace should be easy. After all, we have more ways to reach each other than ever before: voice mail and e-mail as well as old standbys like group meetings, memos, and one-on-one conversations. But, unfortunately, *more* communication doesn't necessarily mean *better* communication. Consider the following case study:

■ Betsy decided that she and her staff should communicate more, so she instituted a weekly meeting. She saw the weekly meeting as her department's primary communication tool–the time when everyone would have the chance to share new information and updates. But after a few months, Betsy learned that her staff didn't like the regular meetings. She couldn't understand their responses—after all, they were communicating! What was the problem? she asked. She was surprised at their responses:

- Regular hours at the company were 8:30–5:00. Betsy had been starting her meeting at 8:00 on Mondays to get a jump on the day and week. This forced employees to arrive early, disregarding kids' day-care and school schedules. She was trying to communicate with her staff on what turned out to be their most stressful morning of the week— and she was causing the stress.

- By insisting that the weekly meeting be her department's primary means of communication, Betsy stifled some flexibility. When employees had new information, they often held it until the weekly meeting rather than sharing it spontaneously. This meant that some employees were late in receiving information they needed.

- The weekly meetings themselves went on for an hour. This was too long for most staff members—they generally stopped paying attention about halfway through.

- Staff members also felt that the meetings were too one-sided. Betsy took most of the time delivering her information to her staff, but she left little time for staff members to share information or ask questions. Staff members felt that no one cared about their concerns, and they wished that they could hold a second weekly meeting—without Betsy.

Though Betsy was attempting to communicate regularly with her employees, that communication obviously wasn't succeeding. Betsy's employees needed information more quickly than she was providing it, and they needed to meet with each other when they were less stressed and could concentrate. They also needed the opportunity to express their own ideas and opinions.

Managers don't always know employees' communication needs.

As Betsy's example points out, managers don't always know employees' communication needs. How can you find out? The best way is to ask them. Some questions you might consider include:

6

- Do you feel well-informed about what's going on in our department? In the organization as a whole?

- Are you receiving information often enough?

- Are you receiving information quickly enough?

- Do you feel that you have a chance to express your thoughts and ideas?

- Do you have any suggestions for how we might improve communication in our department?

Your next step is to determine how you can use all the means of communication available to you to meet these needs. To return to our previous example, Betsy could have met her employees' needs by using voice mail and e-mail to keep people informed of important new developments, rescheduling her staff meetings for later in the day, and giving employees more time to speak during the meetings.

Take a Moment

How do you think your employees would answer the previous questions? List your answers below:

_____

_____

_____

_____

_____

_____

_____

_____

Now have your employees answer the questions and compare your answers. How accurately did you predict their responses?

Visit Employee Work Areas

■ "I just don't know what to do about this client," Geraldo confessed to his friend Tania. "He's making so many demands, and it's getting unreasonable."

"Why don't you tell your supervisor about it?" Tania responded. "Maybe he can help you think of something."

"I don't think he'd understand," Geraldo said sadly. "He spends so much time locked up in his office. I don't think he even understands what we do, and I don't really know him well enough to feel comfortable taking a problem like this to him."

We've seen how important it is for managers to get to know their employees in order to be able to offer effective rewards and reinforcement. The fact that a manager takes time to visit with employees can inspire motivation. But managers who remain isolated in their offices will never get to know their employees. To truly understand your staff and what they do, you need to spend some time with them in their own work areas.

> **The fact that a manager takes time to visit with employees can inspire motivation.**

This principle has been called "Manage by Walking Around" (MBWA), though some managers' eyes now glaze over when they hear that term. Though it may sound simple, MBWA involves much more than simple walking. Effective MBWA means taking the time to talk with employees and actively listen to their concerns. To get the most from your MBWA time, follow these guidelines:

6

◆ **Be considerate of your employees' work schedules.** MBWA shouldn't be intrusive or interruptive. If an employee seems particularly busy, greet that person briefly and move on. Save in-depth conversation for another day.

◆ **Use your MBWA time for constructive enlightenment, not criticism.** It's not a time to reprimand employees for loud radios or messy offices. Employees will resent your visits if they perceive you as a scolding parent.

◆ **Allow enough time for MBWA.** Effective MBWA means taking the time to listen to employees and respond with authenticity. If you're in a hurry, these things can't happen.

◆ **Don't make a big show of MBWA.** You don't have to announce that you're going to start doing it—just gradually weave it into your work style.

◆ **Don't limit MBWA to your subordinates.** It's a helpful process for working with your peers and your own boss, though your style of MBWA will be different in these situations.

◆ **Adjust your amount of MBWA to your employees' preferences.** If you get the impression that your employees find your MBWA burdensome, condescending, or interruptive, and you truly can't find anything you've done wrong, find another means to communicate with them. Don't completely stop visiting others. Just devote more time and energy to other types of communication.

Of course, the nature of your work environment will affect your MBWA efforts. A busy, noisy factory with high production quotas won't be as conducive to MBWA as a quiet office setting. This doesn't mean that you shouldn't use MBWA, but it does mean that you should adjust the length and timing of your visits and support MBWA with other types of communication.

Though it may not be possible to meet in person with telecommuters, managers should not ignore these workers.

One work situation that poses a special communication challenge for the manager is the telecommuting employee. Without ongoing contact with a manager, telecommuting employees may feel isolated and out of touch. Though it may not be possible to meet in person with telecommuters, managers should not ignore these workers. Compensate for the lack of face-to-face contact with frequent phone conversations and e-mail, and invite these employees to visit your office setting whenever possible.

Take a Moment

How often do you visit your employees in their work areas during a typical week? Do you visit some employees more than others? If you aren't visiting all of them regularly, develop a plan for working regular visits into your work schedule.

Listen to Employee Concerns

■ "I think this old PC has just about had it," Sung Li said as she looked at the ancient computer at her company's front desk. "When it crashes, they'll lose a lot of data."

"Shouldn't you tell the boss?" Khan asked. "Then she could get us another hard drive, so we could transfer the information before we lose it."

"Why bother?" Sung Li said. "She never listens to me anyway."

Don't let communication with your employees become a one-way street. Support their motivation by actively listening to their concerns. Some strategies for improving your listening skills include:

◆ **Listening actively when employees speak with you in person.** You may tell employees that you have an "open door" policy, but how do you react to them when they walk in that door? Active listening means giving speakers your undivided attention, not finishing up paperwork or planning your next meeting while they talk. Use nonverbal communication to show that you're paying attention: maintain eye contact with the person speaking, nod to show that you understand what's being said, and ask questions when you don't understand. If possible, come out from behind your desk and take a seat next to the employee so that the two of you can sit at the same level, and remember to put the employee at ease by smiling.

◆ **Providing communication alternatives.** Some employees feel perfectly comfortable bringing up their concerns at a weekly staff meeting, some prefer a private meeting, and others prefer to avoid a meeting altogether and voice their concerns in writing. Provide employees with a variety of means to communicate with you. Some ideas include:

• *Designing a quarterly survey that employees can answer anonymously.* Make sure to include essay-type questions, or a general area for comments so that employees don't feel that their responses are limited to multiple-choice questions designed by you.

> Don't let communication with your employees become a one-way street.

6

- *Offering a suggestion box.* Though some management consultants recommend eliminating this old standby, others believe that it remains a useful communication tool if employees know that they can also bring concerns to you in person.

- *Creating peer feedback teams.* An employee might feel more comfortable discussing some issues with a peer rather than a manager. Give them the opportunity by setting up peer feedback teams.

  TIP: If you start a peer feedback team, train team members so that they will be prepared to handle various types of complaints, and discuss how issues should be brought to your attention without violating employee confidentiality.

◆ **Responding to employees' ideas and opinions.** Employees need to know that the ideas and opinions they express to you don't just disappear into a black hole. Try to act on employee suggestions when possible, and when you aren't able to act, let employees know why. Respond to employees by following up with them individually, or if the issue is a public one, addressing them during a meeting or through a memo or newsletter article.

Maintain the trust of your employees by answering their concerns with honest responses.

◆ **Showing employees that they can trust you.** Trust is vital to open communication. Maintain the trust of your employees by answering their concerns with honest responses and by making sure that confidential communication remains private.

Take a Moment

What alternatives do you currently provide for employees who want to communicate with you? List them below:

_____

_____

_____

_____

What other means of communicating with you could you offer employees?

_____

_____

_____

_____

6

Accept Constructive Feedback

"I don't want any complaining." Our parents might have used this phrase when it was our turn to do the dishes, but it's not a useful attitude for a manager to take into the workplace. To remain motivated, your employees need to be able to tell you when things in your department aren't running smoothly and offer their suggestions for improvement. Don't think of these comments as complaints; think of them as constructive feedback.

Don't think of employee comments as complaints; think of them as constructive feedback.

As a manager, you need to be able to accept employee feedback gracefully and to distinguish between an employee with legitimate constructive feedback and someone who's just letting off steam. How can you tell the difference?

What Is Constructive Feedback?

True constructive feedback deals with something that can be identified and measured in some way. If Mike says, "Things aren't fair around here," and cannot specifically name some instances, he's probably just letting off steam. Maybe Mike thinks the fact that supervisors get paid more than he does "just isn't fair."

Constructive feedback deals with something that can be identified and measured in some way.

But if Saul says, "It's hard to process these claims and be accurate," and then explains that he can't meet his quota because he doesn't receive paperwork from the branch office on time, he has legitimate constructive feedback.

Some employees may find it difficult to give you constructive feedback because they believe that it's wrong to "complain." Discuss with these people the ways that corrective feedback can help your entire department, and let your whole staff know that you always welcome open communication—whether it's seen as positive or corrective.

What about the chronic complainers who are just letting off steam? You can help them become constructive critics by following these steps:

◆ **Help your workers understand the difference between corrective feedback and letting off steam.** Let them know that true feedback will be taken seriously.

♦ **Stress that pointing out a problem isn't enough.** Employees also need to be part of the solution. Encourage workers to suggest a solution when they bring you corrective feedback.

♦ **Let workers know that they need to continue to do their best while the situation is being evaluated and possibly improved.** Work shouldn't grind to a halt just because a problem exists.

Take a Moment

When was the last time an employee in your department gave you constructive feedback about some aspect of your department that needed improvement? How did you respond? Would you respond differently today?

_____

_____

_____

_____

_____

6

Open Communication Shows Respect

When you make the effort to develop open communication with your employees, you show them that you respect them and their contributions to the organization. When employees understand what's happening in their organization and their department and are able to make their ideas and opinions known, they believe that their work is valued, and this helps build their motivation. Strive each day to communicate effectively with your employees and watch your department's performance improve.

Summary

Maintaining open communication with your employees helps inspire and maintain their motivation. Truly open communication involves a number of factors, including:

◆ **Communicating regularly with employees in ways that meet their needs**—When employees feel uninformed and ignored, they often believe that their contribution to the organization isn't valued, which discourages their motivation. You can support strong motivation by providing your employees with information about what's going on in the organization and department and by choosing methods of communicating that are appropriate to their needs.

◆ **Visiting employees in their work areas**—Get to know your employees by visiting them in their work areas, or Manage by Walking Around (MBWA). Use your MBWA time as a chance to learn more about your employees, not to correct them, and plan your visits, so they aren't bothersome or disruptive.

◆ **Listening to employee concerns**—Practice active listening whenever you meet with an employee. Use nonverbal communication to show that the person speaking has your undivided attention. Provide alternative channels for employees to communicate with you, such as a suggestion box or peer feedback committee, and regularly respond to issues raised.

◆ **Accepting corrective feedback from employees**—When employees bring up issues within your department that need improvement, look on their comments as constructive feedback rather than complaints. Help employees understand the difference between corrective feedback regarding something identifiable and measurable and just letting off steam, and encourage them to present solutions along with their feedback.

Self-Check: Chapter 6 Review

Answers to these questions appear on page 110.

1. What is one of the best ways for managers to find out what their employees communication needs are?

   _____

   _____

2. MBWA stands for _____.

3. Effective MBWA involves taking the time to talk with employees and

   _____

   _____.

4. Two strategies that will help you listen more effectively to employee concerns are:

   a. _____

   b. _____

5. Don't think of employee comments as complaints; think of them as

   _____.

6

Chapter*Seven*

Dealing with Unmotivated Employees

Chapter Objectives

▶ Recognize factors that can lead to poor employee performance.

▶ Understand what a manager can do to help unmotivated employees.

▶ Try new techniques to inspire motivation.

M ost of us have heard the phrase "an unmotivated employee" before. But what does it really mean?

Motivation itself is an internal state.

■ Suki looked at her watch and shook her head. James had missed another deadline—the third in as many weeks. Why couldn't he get his work done on time? "I guess he's just not motivated," she thought.

As we discussed earlier, motivation itself is an internal state— how can you know what an employee is or isn't feeling? The fact is, you can't, unless that person tells you.

Why Employees Perform Poorly

Usually, when we believe that an employee is unmotivated, we base our conclusion on the quality of that person's job performance—poor job performance equals lack of motivation. But are we correct in that assumption? After all, many things besides motivation can affect job performance. Poor job performance may be caused by a number of factors, including:

> **Many things besides motivation can affect job performance.**

◆ The employee doesn't understand the expectations for performance.

◆ The employee doesn't have the skills to meet the expectations.

◆ The employee doesn't have the time or resources to do the job properly.

◆ The employee is capable of meeting expectations but isn't motivated to do so.

◆ The expectations for performance are so high that nobody could meet them.

Learning the Cause of a Performance Problem

How can you discover which of these is the cause of a worker's performance problem? The best way is to have a talk with your employee.

Schedule a meeting with the employee in which you describe the ways in which the employee is not meeting your performance expectations. Ask the employee why he or she thinks this is happening, then let the employee respond. You might be surprised by what you learn. Often, employees realize that a problem exists but don't know what to do about it, and they are relieved to have a chance to explain their side of things. The opportunity to work with you to solve the problem will in itself help strengthen the employee's motivation.

As you speak with the employee, you may find that she or he might be motivated to achieve in other circumstances but is not currently in the right job. Perhaps the person is most

7

comfortable working independently but must now work with a team, or perhaps you're asking a team-oriented person to work alone. Perhaps the employee is overqualified and is simply not challenged by the position, or perhaps the job is beyond the employee's skills and abilities.

At that point, you must make a personnel decision—offer training to the employee to bring him or her up to speed, move that person to other job duties, or if there is no other alternative, terminate him or her.

Take a Moment

Think of an employee who is not meeting your expectations for performance. Based on the list given earlier, can you think of an explanation for that person's poor performance? Write it below:

_____

_____

_____

_____

_____

Dealing with Poor Motivation

If you have considered other alternatives and can find no reason for an employee's poor performance, lack of motivation could be the answer. There are many reasons why an employee might not be motivated. You can help solve some of these situations but not all of them.

What Can a Manager Do?

As a first step toward helping an employee with low motivation, ask yourself if you are doing everything you can do as a manager to inspire motivation. Perhaps you haven't conveyed your vision in a way that the employee understands, or maybe you haven't offered a reward that the employee values. Review the previous chapters of this book for more ideas.

Ask yourself if you are doing everything you can do as a manager to inspire motivation.

Take a Moment

Are you doing all you can to inspire motivation in your less-motivated employees? Review the following checklist:

Do I . . .

_____ Articulate a clear vision for my department or team?

_____ Help my employees determine strategic imperatives to meet our goals?

_____ Measure and evaluate my employees' work in a meaningful way?

_____ Recognize employee achievement through a fair reward system?

_____ Tell employees what they need to do in order to earn rewards?

_____ Offer rewards that my employees value?

_____ Use positive reinforcement instead of negative reinforcement or punishment?

_____ Do what I can to create an employee-friendly organizational culture?

7

Even a manager who does everything possible to support motivation may still encounter problem employees. Remember that individuals are ultimately responsible for their own motivation. If an employee stubbornly decides that he or she hates a job or doesn't care about performance standards, a manager's only choice may be termination.

Employee motivation can also be affected by personal factors outside the workplace, including:

◆ Money problems.

◆ Illness or loss of a family member.

◆ Family or marital conflict.

◆ Drug, alcohol, or gambling addiction(s).

◆ Physical illness.

◆ Chronic depression.

As a manager, it is not your role to counsel employees on personal issues.

As a manager, it is not your role to counsel employees on personal issues. However, if you learn or have reason to believe that an outside problem is affecting an employee, you can suggest that she or he seek professional assistance. Many organizations have assistance programs to which you can refer an employee for confidential counseling. Check with your human resources department to see what your organization offers.

Remember Your Responsibilities

Though you may sympathize with a troubled employee, remember that you have a responsibility to your organization and your team to be sure that all employees maintain high levels of performance. An employee who is consistently unable to meet performance standards—for whatever reason—will keep your team from meeting its goals and discourage the motivation of other team members. Remember to document all employee performance problems according to your organization's procedures so that you will be able to defend a termination should one become necessary.

Will firing a poorly performing employee destroy the motivation of the rest of your team? Almost never, if you follow proper procedures and keep the situation as professional as possible. The remaining employees were probably aware of the problem and will understand your decision. If the terminated employee was difficult to work with, they may even be relieved.

Of course, prevention is better than having to deal with employees in this extreme manner. You can't prevent all personnel problems, since people themselves are unpredictable, but making sound hiring decisions and assigning workers to jobs that fit their abilities will greatly increase your chances of motivational success.

Take a Moment

Do you know your organization's procedures for disciplinary action and termination? Don't wait until a problem arises to find out. Visit your human resources department (or whatever department in your organization is responsible for hiring) and find out what the policy is. If they have printed guidelines, request a copy for your files.

7

More Ideas for Inspiring Motivation

Try these additional steps to enhance your workers' abilities to be productive staff members:

- **If possible, eliminate some of the signs of status difference in the office.** Can you make door nameplates the same size? eliminate reserved parking spaces? do away with a separate executive break room? For some organizations, these and other steps would work and be of help to staff members.

- **Can you also eliminate the signs of distrust around your company, such as time cards, time clocks, sign-in sheets, etc.?**

- **Don't avoid employees' "tough" questions.** If you don't answer questions about possible downsizing, layoffs, and other controversial issues, the gossip mill will. Tough questions don't go away; they only get tougher and meatier until they're dealt with.

> If you don't answer questions about controversial issues, the gossip mill will.

- **In establishing rapport with employees, don't get too close or be too distant.** It's not an easy place to get to, since it's a fine line. But going too far in either direction spells trouble.

- **Develop an attitude that you work as much for your employees as they work for you.** Ask your team members how you can help them do their jobs better. Let them know that you are there to help.

- **Celebrate important anniversaries with your employees.** Recognize a new employee's first day by introducing the new worker to the staff, having refreshments, taking the new person to lunch—whatever you can do to make the day special. Also recognize employees on their birthdays and on their work anniversary dates.

- **Make tasks less boring any time you can.** Split up the boring or grunt work. Don't give it all to the one department member who is fresh out of college. What a way to tell someone, "Here's the start of your career."

◆ **Encourage cross-training whenever you can.** In today's ever-changing workplace, cross-training almost always comes in handy.

◆ **Take action now.** Don't start practicing the ideas in this book next week, "when there'll be less to do." You'll keep putting the whole thing, or at least part of it, off until there is a "better" time. Even if you're having difficulty right now with staff members who are gobbling up your time, begin taking measures to inspire motivation.

Practice the principles in this book and augment them with additional knowledge about drawing out the higher and better qualities inherent in all people, and you'll be rewarded handsomely with a loyal staff of hard workers—a group who will make you proud and who will, in turn, hold you in high esteem.

7

Summary

Many factors can affect employee performance, including:

- The employee doesn't understand the expectations for performance.

- The employee doesn't have the skills to meet the expectations.

- The employee doesn't have the time or resources to do the job properly.

- The employee is capable of meeting expectations but isn't motivated to do so.

- The expectations for performance are so high that nobody could meet them.

The best way to determine the cause of poor performance is to discuss the problem with the employee. If you conclude that motivation really is a problem, ask yourself if you are doing everything you can as a manager to inspire and support motivation for this individual. You might try changing the rewards offered or providing more positive reinforcement.

Employee motivation can also be affected by personal factors outside the workplace, including:

- Money problems.

- Illness or loss of a family member.

- Family or marital conflict.

- Drug, alcohol, or gambling addiction(s).

- Physical illness.

- Chronic depression.

An employee who is consistently unable to meet performance standards—for whatever reason—will keep your team from meeting its goals and discourage the motivation of other team members. Remember to document all employee performance problems according to your organization's procedures so that you will be able to defend a termination if necessary.

Self-Check: Chapter 7 Review

Answers to these questions appear on page 110.

1. Lack of motivation is not the only cause of poor employee performance. List four others.

   a. _____.

   b. _____.

   c. _____.

   d. _____.

2. List three personal factors that can affect employee motivation.

   a._____

   b._____

   c._____

3. True or false?
   Individuals are ultimately responsible for their own motivation.

4. True or false?
   It is your duty as a manager to counsel employees on personal issues when those issues affect their workplace performance.

5. True or false?
   Firing a poorly performing employee will destroy the motivation of the rest of your team.

7

Chapter 1

1. False—Managers can only create a work environment that encourages and supports motivation on the part of employees.
2. Money
3. False—Fear is not an effective way to encourage motivation.
4. Hectic
5. Team situations can inspire employee motivation when employees are able to build a strong team relationship and a shared sense of commitment. They can discourage employee motivation when the team experiences a number of conflicts or if individual members believe that their efforts are ignored or undervalued.

Chapter 2

1. Physical/Physiological
   Safety/Security
   Love/Social
   Ego/Status
   Self-Actualization
2. Our incomes can help us buy basic necessities like food and clothing. Our workplace itself can provide us with a clean, comfortable work environment.
3. By giving us the opportunity to work in teams and participate in group activities.
4. Affiliation
   Achievement
   Power
5. They might not have a great need for money, or they might place more value on other factors, such as integrity or personal expression.

Chapter 3

1. A vision or mission statement articulates the results you hope your department will achieve in a way that will inspire your employees.
2. Strategic imperatives are limited, specific goals that employees can complete and measure.
3. Job measures quantify the improvements in job performance that increased motivation can bring.
4. c—Employees should have authority, but they should also be held accountable.
5. Respect for others
   Honesty and integrity
   Fairness

Chapter 4

1. False—An employee must value a reward in order for it to be effective.
2. True—A reward can be effective only if an employee sees it as attainable.
3. d—Workers should never have specific information about the salaries of coworkers and managers.
4. False—You should focus on employee performance only.
5. a. Be as fair as possible in your distribution of rewards.
   b. Monitor employee performance and recognize hard work on the part of all employees.
   c. Find ways to recognize smaller accomplishments as well as larger ones.
   d. Set reasonable performance standards for rewards and regularly let all employees know how they can reach them.

Chapter 5

Take a Moment, page 72

1. NR
2. PR
3. P
4. NR

Chapter Review

1. c—Positive reinforcement
   a—Negative reinforcement
   b—Punishment
2. By building a workplace climate of fear and distrust in which workers feel their job security is threatened
3. By getting to know their employees and their individual preferences
4. b—A friendly corporate culture offers employees the flexibility to deal with family issues.
5. The amount of social time you spend together

Chapter 6

1. Ask them
2. Manage by Walking Around
3. Actively listen to employees' concerns
4. a. Listen actively when employees speak with you in person.
   b. Provide communication alternatives.
5. Constructive feedback

Chapter 7

1. a. The employee doesn't understand expectations for performance.
   b. The employee doesn't have the skills to meet the expectations.
   c. The employee doesn't have the time or resources to do the job properly.
   d. The expectations are so high that no one could meet them.

2. Choose from:
   a. Money problems
   b. Illness or loss of a family member
   c. Family or marital conflict
   d. Drug, alcohol, or gambling addiction(s)
   e. Physical illness
   f. Chronic depression

3. True—Individuals are ultimately responsible for their own motivation.

4. False—You should refer your employee to a trained professional counselor.

5. False—Firing a poorly performing employee will almost never destroy the motivation of the rest of your team.

NOTES

NOTES